## AFFLICTED BUT
## NOT FORGOTTEN

# The Voice
of the Martyrs

*with Renee Dylan*

Living Sacrifice Book Company
Bartlesville, OK 74005

**Sudan: Afflicted But Not Forgotten**

Living Sacrifice Book Company
P.O. Box 2273
Bartlesville, OK 74005-2273

ISBN 978-0-88264-026-6

Edited by Lynn Copeland

Cover design by Lookout Design

Cover creation, page design, and layout by Genesis Group

Printed in the United States of America

Unless otherwise indicated, Scripture references are from the *New King James* version, © 1979, 1980, 1982 by Thomas Nelson Inc., Publishers, Nashville, Tennessee.

"To Sing and Dance in Suffering" has been adapted from *Daughters of Hope: Stories of Witness & Courage in the Face of Persecution* by Kay Marshall Strom and Michele Rickett. Copyright © 2003 by Kay Marshall Strom and Michele Rickett. Used by permission of InterVarsity Press, P.O. Box 1400, Downers Grove, IL 60515. www.ivpress.com.

*"Who shall separate us from the love of Christ? Shall tribulation, or distress, or persecution, or famine, or nakedness, or peril, or sword? As it is written: 'For Your sake we are killed all day long; we are accounted as sheep for the slaughter.' Yet in all these things we are more than conquerors through Him who loved us. For I am persuaded that neither death nor life, nor angels nor principalities nor powers, nor things present nor things to come, nor height nor depth, nor any other created thing, shall be able to separate us from the love of God which is in Christ Jesus our Lord."*

—ROMANS 8:35–39

*"Whenever there is oppression and persecution the Church flourishes. People have to make a fundamental choice—I'm in or I'm out; either I will take my faith seriously and struggle to be a good Christian, or I will leave the faith altogether. Most in Sudan have opted in. It is just like purifying gold in a fire."*

—BISHOP MACRAM MAX GASSIS OF SUDAN, 1998

# SUDAN

## CONTENTS

# ACKNOWLEDGMENTS

This book would not have been possible without the guidance, encouragement, and involvement of many individuals.

I am grateful to Riley K. Smith, who was a helpful advisor, observant editor, and generous source of support from first to final draft. Thank you for seeing me through this process with patience and with such passion for bringing the message of the suffering Sudanese Church to others.

I am thankful for Lynn Copeland, whose fine attention to detail and accuracy greatly enhanced this project with clarity of voice and vision.

I deeply appreciate the staff of The Voice of the Martyrs and am blessed to be able to serve alongside them in raising awareness and support for the persecuted worldwide.

I am blessed, also, by my friends and family, whose love and support accompanied me on this journey. You are gifts of grace.

I thank my heavenly Father for allowing me to encounter the sacrifices of our suffering family in Sudan. I am humbled by their persevering faith, which so powerfully speaks to God's mercy and strength working through us all.

And my heartfelt thanks to you, readers, for opening yourselves up to the trials facing so many of our brothers and sisters in Sudan. It is my hope that this book will somehow assist you in remembering those in chains and serve you well in your own walks of obedience to Christ. I pray we will all continue to rejoice in the fellowship of His saints.

Grace and peace to you,

RENEE DYLAN

# INTRODUCTION:
# THE FIRST SUDANESE CHRISTIAN

*"Now an angel of the Lord spoke to Philip, saying, 'Arise and go toward the south along the road which goes down from Jerusalem to Gaza.'"*
—ACTS 8:26

The year A.D. 37 was a dangerous time to be a Christian. A righteous man, Stephen, had been martyred—stoned to death for proclaiming Christ—about three years earlier. Persecution had broken out against the Church, with a man named Saul, intent on its destruction, going from house to house capturing Christians and throwing them in prison. Believers were scattered throughout Judea and Samaria, except for the apostles, and worked to spread God's Word wherever they fled.

Acts 8 tells of Philip evangelizing in Samaria, with many responding to his message of the Messiah. But his path was to be interrupted. An angel appeared to him and told him to take another path: a desert road. Philip obeyed. On his way he met an Ethiopian, a eunuch who was an important official in the court of Candace, queen of Ethiopia, a region that is now part of North Sudan. (Candace is actually not a name, but a form of

"Kandake," an official title for queens—similar to the use of "Pharaoh" or "Caesar.")

The eunuch was reading aloud this messianic prophecy from Isaiah 53:7,8:

> "He was led as a sheep to the slaughter;
> And as a lamb before its shearer is silent,
> So He opened not His mouth.
> In His humiliation His justice was taken
>     away,
> And who will declare His generation?
> For His life is taken from the earth."
> (Acts 8:32,33)

Philip ran up to the chariot and asked the eunuch, "Do you understand what you are reading?"

"How can I," replied the eunuch, "unless someone guides me?" So he invited Philip to come up and sit with him in his chariot. "I ask you, of whom does the prophet say this, of himself or of some other man?" he asked him. Then Philip shared with him the good news of Christ.

Upon hearing this news, the eunuch pulled his chariot to a halt and asked Philip if he could be baptized. So Philip went down into the water with the eunuch and baptized him.

This is the story of the first recorded Christian from the area that would become Sudan. One can assume that a Christian community grew out of this man's conversion. Some records refer to him as "the first evangelizer of Sudan," stating that he returned to Ethiopia to preach under the penalty of death—as was the danger at the time. In any case, his powerful story speaks of God's truth and love taking root in the heart of the man who would bear the gospel message to his home country—a man who, after coming to know the Messiah, "went on his way rejoicing."

## The Kingdom of Ethiopia

The nation of Sudan has a rich biblical history. In the Scriptures, the Egyptian name for the country directly south of Egypt, along the Nile River, is "Cush" (or "Kush"). This is the region of the world we call Sudan today. It was also referred to as "Nubia" and "Ethiopia" (the African nation now identified as Ethiopia was known by the name "Abyssinia" until the 1920s).

A prophecy against Ethiopia can be found in Isaiah 18. The passage describes a "land the rivers divided"—speaking of the Nile River which runs through the country—that is populated by a people "tall and smooth of skin." The prophetic tone is one of woe—of immense strife and struggle predicted:

> "Woe to the land shadowed with buzzing wings, which is beyond the rivers of Ethiopia, which sends ambassadors by sea, even in vessels of reed on the waters…He

will both cut off the sprigs with pruning hooks and take away and cut down the branches. They will be left together for the mountain birds of prey and for the beasts of the earth; the birds of prey will summer on them, and all the beasts of the earth will winter on them." (Isaiah 18:1–6)

It is hard to read such words without images of modern Sudan coming to mind—images of a nation engulfed in a seemingly endless state of war. But there is more here than an image of war; there is an image of a God who is with His children in Cush, and who remains with them today in the nation of Sudan. A God with His people, always, even those who feel abandoned and forgotten. Isaiah 18:4 records the words of the LORD: "I will take My rest, and I will look from My dwelling place like clear heat in sunshine, like a cloud of dew in the heat of harvest."

The Messiah who captured the heart of the eunuch is the same Messiah to whom people in Sudan are responding today—and with great fortitude and dedication. The story of Sudan's suffering Church is a story of faithful obedience, bringing into reality another important biblical passage about this vast African land: "Ethiopia will quickly stretch out her hands to God" (Psalm 68:31).

## SUDAN TODAY:
## HOPE IN THE MASTER:
## A CAMEL BOY'S STORY

In the late 1990s, seven-year-old Damare Garang was a Christian boy in captivity. He was also a camel boy, a task his Muslim captors had forced him to take on. Though he knew nothing about camels, he feared he would be beaten if he did not comply.

Islamic soldiers captured Damare when his village in South Sudan was attacked, and they sold him as a slave to a Muslim family. One day, one of the camels under Damare's care got away. When his household master heard the news, he glared at Damare and said, "How could you do this? You will surely have to pay! You stupid slave, I should just kill you now." The threats were written all over his master's face, but something seemed to restrain him as his raging eyes bore into the frightened Damare.

Damare was thankful that he had escaped his master's wrath—at least for the moment. The following day he sneaked away to a small church service across the village. Damare was raised in a Christian family, and even at his tender young age, he desired to have fellowship with other Christians and worship his real Master, Jesus. When the slave boy returned to tending the camels, his master was waiting for him. "Where have you been?" he demanded. Partly out of fear—and partly because he didn't have another quick answer—Damare told his master the truth: he had been "to church."

*Damare Garang*

"You have made two grave mistakes," the now irate master began. "Yesterday you lost one of my camels, and today you worship with infidels!" Damare knew there would be no escape.

The master turned and walked into the barn, then quickly returned with a large board, several rusty spikes, and a hammer. Frozen in fear, Damare was dragged out to the edge of his master's compound where he was forced to the ground with his legs over the board. The savage brutality of the master was unleashed as he proceeded to nail Damare's legs to the board, driving nails into his knees and feet to fasten them into the wood. Damare screamed in agony, crying out for help. But his master, silent, simply walked away.

While Damare lay screaming in the field, a man happened to walk nearby. When his eyes fell on the small boy, he was horrified. Like the Good Samaritan, the man crept into the compound and carried Damare to the local hospital where the nails and board were removed. Seven days later the boy was released into the custody of the kind man.

A year and a half later, Damare and the man who saved him were in a village that came under attack, and they were separated. After the defense forces managed to drive away the Islamic soldiers, Damare was left standing alone. But when the commander heard him speak, he realized that

Damare was from the Jieng (also called "Dinka") tribe and told the others, "He is one of us."

Damare was brought back to the army's camp where he told his story. The commander, taken aback by the tragic events, set out to see if he could locate any of Damare's relatives. When none could be found, the commander took the former camel boy home and adopted him as his own.

Damare is sad that he cannot run fast like the other boys, but, remarkably, he says he has forgiven the man who nailed his legs to the board. He knows that Jesus was nailed to a cross so that all our sins could be forgiven. His hope for himself and for his country is in the one and only true Master of all—the Lord and Savior, Jesus Christ.

# THE CHRISTIANS OF ANCIENT NUBIA (A.D. 350-12TH CENTURY)

For many centuries, Christianity was prominent in ancient Sudan and the Church withstood multiple attempts by Muslim armies to overthrow the religion. But there were seasons of decline as well as of growth. The prominence would fall, but God's promise to His people would remain steadfast.

In order to trace the Church in Sudan from Christianity's arrival in the first century to its decline in the fifteenth century, it is crucial to understand the dominance of Islam in the centuries that followed, including in the modern day. While it is clear that the decline of Christianity in ancient Nubia was not exclusively due to external forces, such as Muslim invasions, Christianity's collapse created a spiritual void that Islam would eventually come to fill.

Most of the history available today on the Church in Sudan concerns the growth of Christianity in North Sudan, a region which was known as Nubia until 1899. "Nubia" is derived from the Noba people—a nomadic group who came to the area in the fourth century following the conquering of the kingdom of Meroe by the Ethiopian King Ezana. In place of Meroe, three small Nubian kingdoms were established: Nobotia (to the north), Makouria (in the center), and Alwa (to the south).

Many of the early Christians in Nubia belonged to an influx of Egyptian Christians fleeing the persecution of the Roman emperors shortly after the establishment of the three kingdoms. Most of those who embraced Christianity at this time were prominent figures in society such as royal members and intellectuals. Egyptian Christian refugees more easily influenced such figures because they could understand their native language (Arabic). Around 450, a Christian community and church were built in Nubia. In 542, a Monophysite[1] priest from Constantinople, Julian, began to share his beliefs about Christianity in Nubia, accompanied by an Egyptian bishop, Theodore. Julian appears to be the first reported such figure who set out with the intention of preaching his beliefs of Christianity there.

In the late sixth century, A.D. 580, Nubia became the first official Christian kingdom, and Christian culture flourished, including the construction of churches and schools. In 632, however, soon after the death of Mohammed, the founder

---

1 Monophysitism was condemned as heresy for its views on the nature of Jesus Christ. Many of its followers fled to nearby countries and spread their version of Christianity.

of Islam, the climate of general peace was shattered, and the ensuing conflicts took their toll on the Church. By this time, Mohammed and his followers had converted most of Arabia's tribes and people to Islam. His death did not diminish the vigor of his followers to dominate the Middle East, and the Christian community in Nubia was scattered. Islamic armies conquered Egypt in 642 and, just a year later, they began a series of assaults on Nubia in an effort to seize control. Nubia, however, succeeded in warding off their attacks. It was not until the year 652 when a full Muslim invasion extended to the kingdom of Makouria. Structures not protected by walls were damaged and destroyed, including a prominent cathedral in the city of Dongola.

**A Peace Agreement**
After two attempted conquests of Nubia, a peace agreement was established between Muslim Egypt and Christian Nubia in 652, under the rule of Abdullah ibn Sa'ad ibn Abi Sahr. The agreement, called a *Baqt*, a name that allegedly stems from the Egyptian term for "barter" and the Greco-Roman term for "pact," was developed to secure peaceful relations. Through this agreement, which is rare in Islamic law, Nubia was basically deemed independent. It led to a period of peace in which Christian culture could flourish—for a time. From 697–722,

King Merkurios reigned, and his commitment to building the Nubian Church was so strong that many prominent Christians referred to him as "the new Constantine."[2] Many church buildings were constructed under his rule, and the Church was reportedly respected by bordering lands.

But the *Baqt* also further added to the "Arabization" of the kingdom. The agreement prohibited Muslims from buying land or settling in Nubia, and vice versa. Arab Muslims, including migrants (traders and tribesman) were then more motivated to intermarry with the Nubian people. The *Baqt* agreement enabled Nubia to enjoy a lengthy period free of military conquest, and so even though Islam did expand, its expansion was non-violent. However, it came with a cost.

The *Baqt* lasted nearly seven hundred years, making it one of the longest lasting treaties in history. From 750–1150, in particular, Nubia experienced a "golden age" in the flourishing of Christian art and architecture. But how long would this peace and prosperity last? How would God's Kingdom advance, even in an earthly kingdom of broken peace that's no longer called "Christian"? This was the next chapter to be lived out by the Nubian Church, and added to the legacy of God's faithful in ancient Sudan.

---

2 Constantine was the Roman emperor who brought religious freedom to Christians with the Edict of Milan in 313.

## A CHURCH IN DECLINE (12TH-18TH CENTURIES)

The peaceful phase that the *Baqt* agreement fostered between Christians and Muslims in Nubia did come to an end. As for the Nubian Church, it too would see a time of decline and disappearance. But it would later rise again, proving the resiliency of God's Spirit in the land even after many days where it seemed His followers were nowhere to be found.

In 1172, the Church in Nubia met a new aggressor: the Turkish Mamluks. The Mamluks (Arabic for "owned") were a group composed mostly of Turkish, Kurdish, and Circassian slaves. The Mamluks were openly opposed to Christianity. Upon invasion, Mamluk armies attacked Northern Nubia, setting fire to towns, destroying churches, and dispersing people throughout the nation. In 1265 the new ruler of Egypt, Sultan Baybars, launched a military expedition into Nubia, killing many people and taking others captive. In this chaotic time a number of churches were unused and abandoned.

When Mamluk armies conquered the imperial city of Dongola in 1276, Nubia was turned into an Egyptian dependency and placed under the control of the Egyptian government. Nubia

21

was still officially considered Christian at this time, but Islam was advancing in influence at a slow but steady rate.

The stronghold of Islam in Nubia was deepened in the early fourteenth century, when a Muslim prince, Prince Shekanda, ascended to the throne in the city of Dunqulah. The prince was faithful to the Muslim Sultan Baybars, and he soon decreed that all non-Muslim Nubians had to convert to Islam, pay a head tax (called a *jizya* in Islamic law) to redeem themselves, or be killed. Most Nubians paid the tax. Several of them, however, could not afford to pay the amount and so were nominally converted to Islam—a trend that deeply weakened the life and witness of the Nubian Church.

Arabs changed the country's name from Nubia to Sudan—which means "the land of the blacks" —and forced those who refused to convert to Islam to disperse throughout the African interior. Many of those who fled landed in regions that are now part of modern Ethiopia and Libya.

### "They Have Always Persevered as Christians"

The beginning of the fourteenth century is generally regarded as the end of Christian Nubia. There are some records indicating that in 1317 a church in the city of Dongol was allegedly turned into a mosque. (Some research has since called this into question, suggesting that this church was simply turned into a royal palace.) In 1484, the last known Christian king, Joel, was removed from the throne in the kingdom of Datawo.

A missionary to Ethiopia reporting on Sudan in this time said of the people there, "The people are neither Christians, Muslims, or Jews, but they live in the desire of becoming Christians." Such a statement suggests that even the stronghold of Islam was not enough to stop people from seeking Christ—and according to historical records, very few Sudanese converted to Islam in the twelfth to fourteenth centuries. Sadly, however, there were also few who openly professed their faith in Christ.

By 1500, there was little evidence that there had ever been a "golden age" in Sudan. The early days of the century were marked by the intensification of the slave trade and confusion in political and religious authority due to the arrival of groups from other countries. In 1504, a new people group, the Funj, moved into Sudan from the south in response to pressure from a major Nilotic ethnic group (the Shillik). They rapidly established their supremacy, taking over the empire built up by Ottomon Abdallah Jamma and establishing the Funj Sultanate of Sinnar, which ruled the area for three centuries.

The religious beliefs of the Funj had their origins in a blend of Islam, animism, and Christianity, with Islam as the most prominent. There are no reports of Christians making evangelistic efforts to reach the Funj or Arab nomads and help guide them away from Islam—an absence which many believe contributed to the eventual decline of the Church in Nubia. In 1523 the Sennar monarchy, a dynasty ruled by a sultan in North Sudan, officially converted to Islam.

From the middle of the sixteenth century there is little evidence of any kind of unified or vocal Church in Sudan. Although there are a few recorded incidents of Christians converting to Islam, it seems the faithful were only in isolated pockets. A recently discovered document confirms this state of isolation—yet also speaks to the enduring faith of many in this chaotic time. The document, a letter written by an Italian missionary in 1742, describes sixteenth-century Christianity in the village of Tangos, an island in the Nile located in Sudan. It reads: "There are still some Christians; although they have endured many troubles, disturbances, and wars from the Turks, to force them to embrace Mohammedanism, they, even at the cost of their lives, have always persevered as Christians."

While the growing influence of Islam eventually overpowered the Christian Church in Sudan, it is important to note that its decline was not due to external forces alone. Christianity withered and died out because of the Church's isolation and lack of organization. Yes, church buildings were destroyed, but mosques did not necessarily replace them. The Church was isolated from Christians around the world, including its churches in sister nations.

By the 1800s, the Church in ancient Sudan was utterly disconnected from the Church beyond its borders, which only increased its vulnerability to Islam's pressure. But the Church in decline was still a Church—one in which the Spirit of the Lord was at work in Sudan. From these formative days, the faith would not only survive, it would thrive, and God's people would come to be known not for vulnerability, but for spiritual victory.

# THE JIENG TRIBE OF SUDAN:
# SUFFERING, SACRIFICE,
# AND FAITHFULNESS

*"Let us give thanks to the Lord in the day of
devastation, and in the day of contentment."*
—FROM A HYMN WRITTEN BY MARY ALUEEL
GARANG, A JIENG CHRISTIAN

The Jieng (also referred to as the "Dinka") are one
of the largest tribal groups in Southern Sudan.
They have undergone some of the most devastating persecution of all the tribes in Sudan in recent
years, having endured displacement, slavery, and
other such suffering. As the first converts in South
Sudan, they also have a powerful legacy in the
identity of Sudan's Christian Church.

When European Catholic missionaries first
arrived in Sudan in the late nineteenth and early
twentieth centuries, they focused their efforts on
promoting Catholicism among members of the
Jieng tribe. The presence of Protestant Christians
among the Jieng was established in 1906.

The monotheistic beliefs of the Jieng tribe
led missionaries to see them as more open to the
gospel message. For many long years, however,
the Jieng resisted the Christian message. Many
distrusted it as a foreign belief system and were

unwilling to give up cultural practices associated with their tribal heritage (such as polygamy). Some initially "converted" as a strategy against the Arab Muslims—as a means of maintaining the Christian and traditionalist presence in the black African North. Slowly, however, the faith began to take root among the tribe and flourished. It became clear, especially with the emergence of Jieng church leaders, that there was a deep and unique indigenous Christian community in formation.

While the legacy of Jieng Christians is one of suffering, it is also one of incredible overcoming faith. "The first Jieng Christian," in 1882, was a former slave named Salim Wilson. He drew on his experience of liberation from slavery into freedom, from the deception of Islam to God's truth, in his work and witness. He wrote of his enslaved countrymen, "Poor victims of Arab cruelty! There is no peace for them by day: no rest for them by night. Life is a burden, and yet Death flees from them. 'How long, oh Lord?' ask the souls of martyred saints, in the Book of Revelation, as they feel that the divine vengeance due to their persecutor, is so long delayed."

Another liberated Jieng slave, Daniel Deng Sorur, became a teacher at a Christian school and also wrote powerful, poetic laments about being physically enslaved and forcibly converted to Islam.

He was passionate about equipping Sudanese Christians to be active and effective witnesses.

For the first half of the twentieth century, Archibald Shaw, an Anglican gospel pioneer, worked among the Jieng in the town of Bor, South Sudan—a region which had long been resistant to the gospel despite multiple missionary efforts. He had a special compassion for the Jieng people and a passion to help this oppressed people group turn to the Lord and draw on His love in their suffering.

In long decades in which Sudan has been embattled in civil war, Jieng Christians have also been targeted and killed by Arab Muslims of the north, who see them as a threat to Islam's dominion and growth. In 1964, a Jieng priest, Barnabas Deng, was killed in Wau. Other Jieng believers killed around this time included church leaders John Malual, Hendy Mabor Toric, and Gabriel Kolnynin. Such losses strengthened the identification of the Jieng people with the struggle of South Sudan since, in both struggles, the oppression stemmed from the Arab Muslim belief that only those who were of Arabic descent and who professed Islam belong in Sudan.

Muslims from the North have destroyed many Jieng villages in attacks. Even in the hardest years of civil war, many Jieng have accepted Christianity and become creative and confident leaders of the Church in South Sudan.

Marc Nikkel was an American Episcopalian missionary and theological teacher who ministered throughout South Sudan for twenty years, working extensively with the Jieng people. He was beloved by thousands of Sudanese for his compassionate work in equipping Christians with biblical training, celebrating the rich and artistic spirituality of the Sudanese (including hymns and worship songs), and providing practical aid for those suffering due to years of war. Upon Marc's death from cancer at age fifty on September 3, 2000, a friend said these words: "Marc was an apostle to the oppressed and persecuted church. He understood his mission to Sudan through the eyes of Jesus. The theme of God's liberation of the poor and oppressed was always heard in his messages. Jesus Christ the liberator, the helper and the healer of the wounded will restore the scattered diaspora of the Sudanese church. These were the chosen people of God to witness to the living faith of the persecuted church that has grown from the Cross of Christ."

Since the twentieth century, Jieng Christians have made particularly moving and vibrant contributions to the world of worship music, especially in their times of persecution. There are many hymns that reflect their commitment to faith amid adversity—hymns that uniquely reflect the culture of these African believers, and that speak to their belief in an afflicted but victorious Christ whom they've come to know ever more intimately through their trials. Many of these hymns contain vivid sacrificial imagery that exalts Christ, the Lamb who was slain.

The Jieng people have seen much suffering— yet they have also seen the faithfulness of the Lord to His people in enabling the Church not only to survive in times of war, persecution, and uncertainty, but to prosper in faith. They carry with them a legacy of steadfast praise, which has encouraged their fellow believers in Sudan and the Church beyond its borders to look to God in all circumstances and intimately seek Him with praise and supplication.

# NEW PRESSURES: THE MAHDIST ISLAMIC REVOLUTION (19TH CENTURY)

The nineteenth century held sweeping changes for the country and its Christians. Believers, both Sudanese and foreign missionaries, encountered new pressures to deny their belief in God. Those who dared to proclaim the name of the Lord in this time bore witness to the sovereignty of God, even in a land under earthly authorities opposed to their faith.

In 1821, during the Ottoman Empire,[3] a Turkish army invaded Sudan, unifying the Northern region of the country and establishing a Turkish regime. This began the Ottoman period in Sudan, a time often referred to as the "Turkiyah." In this period, ethnic groups were forced from their traditional lands and the practice of exporting Sudanese slaves to Egypt grew. The government encouraged Khatmiyyah, an orthodox religious order of Sufism (a mystical form of Islam).

The late nineteenth century ushered in a period that would prove to be even more challenging for the Christians in Sudan: the Mahdist

---

3 A rule established by southwestern Turks that lasted 1281–1923 and encompassed Anatolia, the Middle East, part of North Africa, and southeastern Europe.

31

Islamist revolution. Sufism proclaims the coming of an "Expected Redeemer" or divine Mahdi ("Messiah"). In 1881, a religious teacher from North Sudan, Mohammed Ahmed, declared himself to be this "Redeemer," chosen by God to restore the nation to the "true religion" of Islam. In so doing he set in motion a brief but powerful period of Islamic insurgency marked by zeal for the "purification" of the nation, by enforcing traditional Islamic ideals through violence. Many Muslims were eager to embrace this "Messiah"

*Mahdi ruler Muhammed Ahmed*

and his quest to rid their religion of the "worldliness" which they believed had drowned out traditional and true Islam.

Ahmed capitalized on the resentment in Sudan over the Turkish-Egyptian government, which many mistrusted due to its foreign nature. He played on fears over the British forces present, implying that they were campaigning to Christianize the nation and overthrow Islam (and that, for example, their efforts to abolish slavery were merely a part of this effort). This led Arab Muslims to openly distrust and resist the British, and fed into their eagerness for a leader who could maintain Islam's supremacy and longevity. In their eyes, Ahmed was such a leader.

Settling in the Nuba Mountains, Ahmed began what is now referred to as the Mahdist Islamic revolution, waging a *jihad* ("holy war") against the Egyptian leaders in Sudan and ending sixty years of Turkish-Egyptian rule. Both European and African Christians, church leaders and members, were imprisoned, some for several years. Many died in captivity. For Sudan's Christian communities the revolution was a time of great turmoil and instability. Under the Mahdist regime many faced severe pressure to turn from Jesus, their true Messiah. Church buildings and mission stations were destroyed and missionaries scattered throughout the region, often relocating to the Upper Nile or the region of Omdurman. By 1881, Mahdist forces targeted the small towns of Malbes and Dilling in central Sudan. Missionaries were expelled by slave traders and captured by the Mahdists.

In 1882, the Mahdi's army captured and imprisoned eight missionaries in Dilling. The missionaries refused to embrace Islam and were about to be executed when, at the last moment, to their surprise, the Mahdi himself intervened on their behalf. The missionaries were held in the Mahdi's camp. Three of them soon died due to sickness acquired during their confinement.

In this time of new pressures, church leaders sought out strategic methods of witnessing. One church leader, Archbishop Francesco Sogaro, ordered missionaries to withdraw from Khartoum and relocate to Cairo. There, the missionaries worked among Sudanese Christian refugees; even captivity did not stop believers from boldly serving God. One church leader, Josef Ohrwalder, was captured in 1885 by Mahdist troops in Kordofan, central Sudan, and served as a leader for other Christian prisoners for years, until he escaped with other missionary captives six years later.

Foreign missionaries faced particularly hard trials during the Mahdist revolution. Even those who were not taken captive faced a new level of isolation from the outside world. While in captivity, these missionaries had no access to financial aid or even proper food; several starved to death. By 1891, at least half of the missionaries in Sudan had perished.

**Everything for Christ**
British General Charles Gordon is heralded as the inspiration of many missions in Sudan. In the late nineteenth century, General Gordon felt a passion and a burden to free the South Sudanese people from the tyranny of slavery by Northern Arab traders. Gordon arrived in Sudan in 1874, intent on overthrowing the slave traders. He was

admired for his zealous Christian faith, respected for his military prowess (including a legacy of military exploits in China nearly a decade earlier), and known for his eccentric and passionate personality, which included a fiery temper. He became the Governor General to the Sudan, commanding British and Egyptian troops in revolt against the Anglo-Egyptian rule upon Britain's order. The Sudanese respected his courage as a warrior, even if some undoubtedly resisted the presence of a British Christian in a position of military authority. For four years he succeeded in redeeming slaves and expelling slave dealers, as well as drawing the attention of the British to the plight of the downtrodden in Sudan.

The last few years of General Gordon's life consisted of attempts to help weaken the Mahdi's military forces. It was this fight that led him to his last battle, however. In February 1884, the Mahdi's forces, their confidence bolstered by a number of successful battles against the British, set their sights on the city of Khartoum as a means of furthering their control. General Gordon traveled to Khartoum and committed his efforts to warding off the attack, believing it to be his duty to defend this city and prevent the Mahdi from gaining more power and authority. The city was heavily guarded by Sudanese and Egyptian troops who, under Gordon's leadership, attempted to defend it. There, after ten months, General Gordon was speared to death by Mahdist soldiers in January 1885.

The Church Missionary Society in England even began a Gordon Memorial Fund after his death—a fund designated for the sending of missionaries to Sudan. He is still referred to affectionately as "General Pasha" by many Sudanese today, and these words of his are often quoted: "A man must give up everything, understand everything, for Christ."

**Years of Oppression**
Along with oppression of black African Christians, the Mahdist revolution also persecuted Coptic Christians who had come from Egypt. (The Coptic Orthodox Church is the oldest and largest church in Egypt.) All Copts were to be pressured to embrace Islam—and even after doing so, many were forced to live in the isolated region of Omdurman. Those who "converted" never seemed to be quite free of suspicion and were marked by having to wear the color black. Coptic girls were forced to marry Mahdist officers, to the horror of their families, especially those who still secretly held to their Christian faith.

In 1885, the Mahdi captured Khartoum in a large-scale siege. Many Coptic believers were murdered and the Coptic church Al Adra was destroyed. Although some Coptic believers did give in to pressure and convert to Islam, others remained secret believers, pretending to embrace Islam but gathering at night for Christian worship. Newcomers to Christ were also baptized in secret. Some Christians professed to be Muslims to save their lives, but secretly worked energetically among the Copts to help them sustain their

The Mahdist State, 1881–98

faith. One such Christian was Abuna Philanthaos, a church leader who also helped to secure the release of several missionary captives from the Mahdist forces.

In June 1885, Ahmed, the supposedly divine Mahdi, fell ill with typhus. To the shock of his followers, he died shortly thereafter at only forty-one years of age. Abdullah al-Ta-aishi was appointed as his successor, serving as a military leader. The strength of his movement was greatly impaired, however, by internal leadership conflicts, and was not to last long.

In a historical battle on September 2, 1898, an army commanded by the British General Sir Herbert Kitchener defeated the forces of al-Ta-aishi's army. Eleven thousand were killed and sixteen thousand wounded in the fight. The rule of al-Ta-aishi was collapsing, and in November of the following year he was killed by the British, putting an end to the Mahdist revolution.

But the influence of this period would live on. The Church had seen the deadly face of Islamic rule and its ability to scatter the faithful. Even as the Mahdist revolution swept the nation, there remained committed followers of Christ with a fervor for ensuring the endurance of the Church. Sudanese Christians continued to respond to the costly call to "give up their everything for Christ," even at the risk of their liberty and life.

## SUDAN TODAY:
## "I HAVE MANAGED TO
## BE FAITHFUL"

*Following is the testimony of Gabriel Tutue, a Christian evangelist who was arrested and tortured by government security officials in Sudan in March 1986.*

During the arrest they tortured me in all ways. They put me between life and death. After torturing, the security [forces] decided I was innocent and they released me while they made further investigations. They called me a rebel. I rejected this word and said I did not know the word "liberation" since I was born. I said to them that I was a Christian. I serve in the Church. If you are torturing me because I am Christian, for sure I am a Christian, and I accept what you are doing. They said that this will not prevent me from being treated like a criminal and they started to practice many ways of torturing me. They beat for me for three hours continuously, they burned my hand with an iron, they cut my fingers with pliers, and they tried to cut my throat.

The senior security officer was present and he ordered them to crucify me in the sun on the army tank. They beat me and tied my legs and hands like on a cross. That was between 1 p.m. and 2 p.m. and the sun was very hot. At last the

officer said that because I did not want to confess
they should bring red pepper to put on my anus so
that I should die. They brought a pipe and they
put red pepper in it. They tried to put this pipe
in my anus but God redirected them and the
pipe did not enter my anus. The officer thought
that the iron pipe had entered and he started to
blow the pepper inside but the pepper poured
out. That torture I can never forget because by it
I have known the power of God. After blowing
they went away, thinking I could die soon, but
nothing happened to me.

The power of evil and God's Spirit began to
struggle within me. The evil spirit said, "You can
confess with a lie and then you will be free." But
at last I encouraged myself and remembered the
scripture, "If you deny me in front of people, I will
deny you in front of my Father and his angels"
and also "Be faithful unto death and I will give
you a crown of life." I became even more coura-
geous when I remembered the incident which
happened to Shadrach, Meshach, and Abednego
when they were thrown into the fire in the Old
Testament. I have managed to be faithful and I
defeated Satan by the power of Jesus Christ.

Source: "Testimony of Gabriel Tutu, Christian Evangelist," in
R. Werner, W. Anderson, and Andrew Wheeler, *Day of Devas-
tation, Day of Contentment: The History of the Sudanese
Church Across 2000 Years* (Nairobi, Paulines Publications
Africa, 2000), 611–12.

## A SUDANESE HYMN
## OF THE JIENG PEOPLE

### "Cover Us"

It is we, O God, it is we, look back upon us,
and bless our days, bless this place,
this land we are in, so that it may be a holy land,
which you chose for us where we worship,
where we work, where your people are taught.
Open the light upon us, here, here.

*Chorus:*
Cover us with your wings
Like a bird covers her chicks;
Embrace us intimately, O God,
hold us intimately
in these bad years,
So that we may have life
through faith in you,
O God.

## ON THE ROAD
## TO INDEPENDENCE
## (1899-1956)

Sudan's road to independence was long and chaotic, characterized by clashes between native and
foreign forces. For Christians in the country, these
were years of evangelistic restrictions, slander cam-
paigns, and other such challenges. Yet ministry
limits and mistruths could not stop the work of the
Church—not entirely. It was a road many walked
with unyielding faith.

Following the fall of the Mahdist rule, several
Christian missionary groups were eager to enter
Sudan. Most Christians, including believers from
Egypt, Ethiopia, and Armenia, had settled in the
Masalma quarter of Omdurman during the Mah-
di's rule, and so missionary groups first set their
sights on restoring the Christian community in
this area.

In 1899, an agreement between Britain and
Egypt established Sudan as under a Condominium (or joint authority). This Anglo-Egyptian
agreement led to restrictive policies on Christian
evangelism in the country. British authorities
feared that missionary activity could spark rebel-
lions from Muslims, as they suspected that Mus-

lims could view Christian missionaries as disruptive troublemakers. Although the government did not prevent missionary activity, strong restrictions were placed on Christian work, including a prohibition of direct evangelism. Missionaries were permitted to do educational and medical work, but they were forbidden to do any activity that could be seen as an attempt to spread the Christian faith among the Muslim people.

During the Condominium period of 1899 to 1955, Christianity had a vibrant presence in the field of education in North Sudan. A number of mission schools were established. Sudanese families were initially hesitant to send their children to these schools. In the 1930s, however, Arab Muslims who opposed Britain's southern policy began strongly advocating for a central national government (in Khartoum) that would function under Islamic law. In light of this wave of nationalism, many parents came to see the possible advantages of a Western education, which could equip their children with practical skills and international knowledge. Many Muslim boys even attended the schools at this time, as parents were eager to raise up children ready to become part of the ruling class, should a centralized government come to be. Education proved to be a powerful sphere in which Christians connect with Muslims and other nonbelievers, even amid a time of restrictions on evangelistic activity.

Sir Francis Reginald Wingate, a British general and administrator in Egypt and the Sudan, was committed to bolstering the Christian faith in South Sudan so that it could stand up to the strong Islamic North. He demonstrated his devotion to the growth of the Church in Sudan by encouraging Christian missionaries to focus their evangelistic efforts on the South rather than the North. However, he imposed restrictions on the movement of these missionaries, allotting them areas in which to work and keeping different missions groups separate to reduce potential territorial tensions between them. Roman Catholic religious groups had established Southern missions before the Mahdist revolution, and they continued their work during the Condominium. Presbyterian and Anglican groups were active as well.

Although the Condominium government altered the ministry climate in the North almost immediately, by imposing new evangelistic restrictions, there was initially very little change in the South. The South was long isolated from the North due to its geography—in particular, a large swamp (the "Sudd") separated the two regions until it was penetrated by military forces in 1839. This geographical divide had lessened the influence of Arabic culture and so Islam had also advanced very little. As with the North, however, Christian missionaries were active in education as well as in other limited special services, including medical clinics, and these positions continued amid the government changes.

## The Southern Policy

In 1930, the Anglo-Egyptian "Southern Policy" was declared—a policy that was intended to isolate South Sudan from the North as well as slow the influence of Islam and Arabism in the South. Many have since concluded that, in regard to curbing the influence of Islam, this policy did more harm than good. While it did succeed in limiting some of Islam's influence, it also deepened the Islamic identity of the North and even led the Arab Muslim majority to dismissively view Sudan's Christian Church as a colonial creation, vulnerable and without a distinctly Sudanese identity. Sadly, it was true that many Christian communities then were quite small and heavily reliant on missionary leadership for their spiritual guidance and religious organization.

In 1946 the "Sudan Administrative Conference," called by the British Governor General of Sudan to determine the participation of the Sudanese people in government, determined that Sudan be administrated as one country. The capital of Sudan was designated to be the Northern

city of Khartoum. Muslims were allowed to pros-
elytize while Christians were still restricted from
doing so. Also, in a further demonstration of the
advance of Arabism and Islamization, Arabic was
introduced as the official language of government administration.

After the 1946 government policy merged
North and South Sudan into a single political
entity, there was nationwide expectation of im-
pending independence from Egypt and Britain's
governing authority. Those in the South, however,
looked toward such independence with great trepi-
dation, some even feeling Britain was abandon-
ing them completely to the North. There were but
a few Southerners in posts of political authority.
As such, the South felt weak to withstand pressure
from the North. Many Southerners viewed the
North's quest for national "unity" as a vehicle for
them to extend complete dominance of Arab culture and the Islamic religion through the whole
country.

The Christian communities in the South and
in the central Nuba Mountains were uncertain as
to whether independence would hinder or help
the growth of the Church. Mostly, they felt ill-
prepared to stand against a Muslim majority. There
were very few church leaders and most of them
had very little theological education due to the
slow pace at which formal education of any kind

was advancing. Could a Christian minority survive, and in fact flourish and grow, in an independent Sudan dominated by Islam? Or was it possible that in such an independent Sudan, the influence of Christianity would decrease—perhaps even die out? It was hard to hear the rumblings about "independence" and "unity" and not worry that they were in fact a guise for religious oppression.

The eve of independence was certainly a time when Sudanese Christians needed to remember to entrust themselves to the Lord, knowing Him as the one to depend on—the rock on which the Church could stand, even if independence made the Christian community feel even more like a small island of true faith in a sea of Islam.

# A NEW TIME OF TRIBULATION:
# THE FIRST CIVIL WAR
# (1955-1972)

The year 1956 brought a new season of suffering to the nation of Sudan: civil war. It was a time of great devastation and challenge, but also a time for the Church to show its resiliency in the face of tremendous pressure to bow to Islam.

In 1954 the Egyptian and British governments had signed a treaty guaranteeing Sudanese independence. But before Sudan could officially enter this independence, it was thrown into civil war. In 1925, during the Anglo-Egyptian Condominium, a Land Act was drafted by British government administrators which, due to influence from their homeland practices, largely granted land on the basis of heritage. As a result, Sudan inherited a semi-feudal legal system of land tenure. In August 1955, Southern armies, fearful of the intensifying marginalization they witnessed by the North reneging on promises of a separate system for the South, mutinied in the small Southern town of Torit. The event, known as "The Torit Mutiny," resulted in the death of hundreds of Northerners stationed in the South. Soon after, Southerners formed a guerrilla army—a separatist group ready to take up armed defense against

48

the Muslim Arab North. By the time British and Egyptian governments declared Sudan independent in January 1956, it was a nation at war.

The nation's military landscape was altered as military rule came into effect in November 1958, when a Northern official and political figure, General El Ferik Ibrahim Abboud, overthrew the civilian government of Abdullah Khalil in a bloodless coup. So began Sudan's first period of official military rule. Abboud was intensely dedicated to expanding Arab and Islamist dominance of the nation—and his government immediately imposed changes and restrictions that led to new challenges for the Church in the South. Mosques and Muslim schools, subsidized by the government, were planted in the region. In February 1960, the traditional Muslim day of prayer, Friday, was made the day of rest throughout the country. Southern schools, in protest of this decision, went on strike and were met with severe penalty, including a church leader who was sentenced to twelve years in prison for distributing a pamphlet criticizing the change of the prayer day.

Perhaps the greatest indications of the fervor of the Muslim North against the Christian South in Sudan were the restrictions placed on missionary activity. In 1962, the Missionary Societies Act established a series of serious controls, including forbidding foreign missionaries to conduct services outside of their church buildings or to erect new church buildings. The Act also forbade them from baptizing children under the age of eighteen without their parents' permission and obligated missionaries to annually apply for an evangelism license from the Council of Ministry. Ambiguity in the wording of the document also allowed the restrictions to be applied beyond foreign missionaries and used to harass the national Sudanese Church. The Arabic word for "missionary" (*qasis*) means "priest" and the Arabic word used for "mission" (*kanisa*) is the word for "church"—thus allowing the restrictions to be more widely applied and used against local church leaders as well as their congregations.

In the years that followed, Islam did not significantly advance in the South. However, the Muslim North was relentless in painting missionaries as troublemakers to be removed by accusing them of causing "disunity" through their activities, which they equated with "introducing and promoting a new civilization and culture different from what are prevailing in other parts of the country." In February 1964, in a bold move, the government expelled all missionaries from the South. The media justified the action, claiming it was not just a move against Christianity but a means of encouraging "unity." Missionaries were accused of aiding the rebels, who were growing stronger in the South and speaking up boldly against Islam. The government eventually issued a Memorandum in defense of the expulsion.

Could the Sudanese Church withstand such a blow? Many feared that its ministry would weaken. It was in this time, however, that the Church was in fact rejuvenated, largely due to the work of dedicated evangelists and leaders. The Church grew in many Southern areas (although there was little growth in nomadic regions). Also, Southern Christians became passionate about cultivating a Christian community that would operate self-sufficiently —that is, relying on their own resources and people, rather than on foreign Christian leadership.

Many of the Christians demonstrated a bold, unwavering passion for Christ in South Sudan during this time in the face of violence. Several believers who stood up against the government's relentless attempts to force Islam on its citizens were tortured. On July 9, 1964, a South Sudanese priest known as Father Sylvester prevented the destruction of the church in Kator by standing directly in front of a tank gun. That same day, the Catholic Bishop of Wau, Ireno Dud, was walking near a river in the city of Juba when government troops opened fire on him in an assassination attempt. He survived the brazen attack, but it was clear that even high-profile religious leaders were at great risk.

Sudan's first civil war was marked by widespread violence, disease, and starvation as conflict escalated between the North and the South. In May 1969, Gaafar Mohammed Numeri seized control of the country in a military coup. The country was then renamed the Democratic Republic of Sudan. Numeri was elected president shortly afterward, a move which cemented the power of a radically Islamic leader.

The next couple of years contained some of the most atrocious and openly hostile attacks on Christians by the government. In July 1970, government troops massacred fifty to sixty Christians—men, women, and children—in a church at Banza, near the Sudan-Congo border. The troops tied the believers together with ropes, led them to the back of the chapel, and fastened them against the pews, with the children seated in front of their parents. They then shot them and set the chapel on fire. Some of the children who were wounded tried to escape from the blazing building, but were caught and thrown back into the flames.

Under Numeri's leadership, significant peace talks began to take place between the North and South, due to mediation efforts sponsored by the World Council of Churches in partnership with Ethiopian Emperor Haile Selassie. In March 1972, these talks led to the signing of a peace accord called the Addis Ababa Agreement (also known as the Addis Ababa Accord) which granted the South autonomy. The civil war was over.

As of 1972, a new season of peace had descended on Sudan. But would it last? As for the Church, the Christian faith had served as a source of inspiration for many struggling for liberation, and the "Christian South" was a fixed characteristic in Sudan's religious shape. But what would the future of the Church look like in Sudan in the years ahead, after seventeen brutal years in which an estimated one and a half million people, most of them Christians, were dead at the hands of Sudan's Islamist government? Only time would tell.

## SUDAN TODAY:
## TO SING AND DANCE
## IN SUFFERING

Dr. Anna Lidu could not turn away from the suffering of her people. Having grown up in war-torn Sudan, she had known, even as a girl, that there were many in the nation enduring great injustice and pain. The civil war had made schooling difficult for nearly everyone, but Dr. Lidu persevered, going on to become a medical doctor. She started a medical practice in the capital city of Khartoum, one of the safest areas to live and work since the second civil war began in 1983. But it was not until she left this stable region to start up the first indigenous women's ministry in Sudan that she was able to see firsthand the tribulations of brothers and sisters displaced by the mass violence of the war, from bombings to burning and massacres of entire towns. Many in the refugee camps were Christians.

The medical needs of those displaced by the war were overwhelming. Their conditions made the camps hotbeds for severe diseases, including meningitis, and many inhabitants suffered the effects of poor nutrition and lack of clean drinking water. It wasn't just their bodies that were broken—many of the people were traumatized from the brutal violence they had experienced. Several had witnessed the killings of loved ones and fellow believers, including Christians who had been lined up and shot in the head with three-inch nails, run over by Soviet-made tanks, and executed at point-blank range. Families in the camp also talked of Muslims carrying off their women and girls and selling them into slavery, which was another tool that the National Islamic Front was using against Christians.

Dr. Lidu also gave medical care to Sudanese Christian women who had been targeted in particularly heinous attacks by Muslims. One woman in the camp had been found on the road, unconscious, with her breasts cut off. The villagers informed her that government forces had been capturing women and asking them if they were Christian or Muslim. If they answered "Muslim" they were freed. If they said "Christian," however, they were raped, mutilated, and left to die on the road, so that those who passed by would see them as a warning against resisting Muslim forces.

"This woman was supposed to be an example to others who would dare to remain Christians," Dr. Lidu said. "But I wish they could have heard her as she was recovering. She spent her time praising the name of Jesus!"

Dr. Lidu's heart ached to see her people suffering in such a way—to see those in the camp literally dying from despair. In an effort to revive hope in the camp, she and her team began holding worship services. Their joyful singing drew people in and crowds grew larger and larger. Together, believers would listen to an encouraging gospel message and share testimonies and pray. They also loved to sing and dance!

"Before the war, singing and dancing was a wonderful part of our worship," said Dr. Lidu. "To bring it back revives the spirit, turning their mourning into dancing. Even the most persecuted, the most destitute people can have the joy and hope of Jesus Christ."

## THE MELUT
## MARTYRS

The year was 1964, nearly a decade after the flame of civil war was first ignited in Sudan. Missionaries had been expelled by the government; Islamists were eager to see Islam dominate and Christianity eradicated. The days ahead looked very troubling indeed, not just for church leaders, but for all followers of Christ in Sudan. Yet in this climate, Christians still dared to speak of God's love and preach His Word—some even when a gun was pointed to their head, like the four men of Melut who would die for Christ.

In the summer of 1963, a mosque had been constructed in the town of Melut in the Upper Nile region of Sudan. From there, the influence of Islam vigorously spread. Those who were caught with a Bible in their home could be killed. It was difficult for Christians to even obtain steady employment. Many churchgoers converted to Islam under the pressure. Believers watched with dismay as their former church members forcibly denied Christ in order to have jobs.

By August, there were very few Christians left in the town. However, five active and passionate church leaders remained: Paul Changjwok, Gideon Adwork, Simon Anyang, William Olyew, and

Daniel Yany. These brave leaders knew the risks of proclaiming Christ but continued to do so, boldly and faithfully.

On the evening of August 15, 1964, three of the men—Gideon, Simon, and William—were gathered in Gideon's home, preparing to eat dinner together as they often did. William, however, was feeling very tired and left for his home. Soldiers eventually surrounded Gideon's house. Gideon went outside first, followed by Simon. The soldiers approached the home and arrested the men. The believers were accused of aiding Southern rebels by allegedly buying provisions for them.

William's wife learned of the arrest of the other men and warned her husband to flee, but he refused. When the soldiers realized William was not at Gideon's house, they sent soldiers to his home to arrest him also.

Three days later, the men were still detained, and no one knew exactly what was going to happen to them. On that day, Paul, the men's friend and fellow leader, remembers hearing the sound of gunshots in the town. First the shots sounded as if they were coming from the mission center, then the forest, then the river. And then, to Paul's horror, he heard shots that sounded different, as if they were hitting another target. These were the shots that brought the lives of the brave leaders—Gideon, Simon, and William—to an end.

It was later learned that, before they were shot, all three of these men were questioned about their ministry. The soldiers demanded to know the names of other Christians involved in their ministry, telling them that they would be shot if they did not cooperate. But these men stood firm, refusing to give up any information. "Do whatever you want to do," they reportedly said, moments before they were killed.

Only the body of Simon was later found by a steamer traveling on the river. They took his body out of the water and asked the local people to identify it. Residents denied they knew who it was, afraid that they would be killed if they admitted to knowing such a well-known Christian.

Paul is certain that if they mentioned his name, he would have been killed, and that the same would have happened to any believer whose identity they revealed. Following the words of John 15:13, "Greater love has no one than this, than to lay down one's life for his friends," they showed what it means to live in complete obedience to Christ, even in a climate of extreme persecution, protecting the witness of other believers in the area.

A theological training college named after Gideon was eventually opened in Melut. The Gideon Theological College has since been moved to Khartoum, and continues to equip and inspire Sudanese Christians to stand for Christ today.

# WARFARE ONCE AGAIN: THE SECOND CIVIL WAR (1983-2005)

Between the end of the first civil war and the beginning of the second civil war was a decade of relative peace. Christian leaders welcomed the level of stability, many of them setting out to fortify mission institutions and church buildings that had been destroyed or closed down in the pandemonium of the first war. One such leader was Daniel Deng Bul, who in 1979 was sent to Port Sudan, a place that was still very hostile to Christian evangelism. Here, Deng aided in developing mission schools, Bible classes, and prayer centers. He said, "Sudan is our country; we must be ready to meet the need of our people by telling the Good News even if Christians are persecuted for their faith."

But the peace was short-lived. In the years leading up to the war, the South was increasingly anxious about the North's failure to implement the promises outlined in the Addis Ababa Agreement established in 1972 to end the first war. This dissatisfaction was at the center of the creation, in May 1983, of the Sudan People's Liberation Movement (SPLM), a rebel political movement, and accompanying rebel group the Sudan People's Liberation Army.

Rumblings of another civil war intensified in line with the development and growing authority of the Muslim Brotherhood. The Muslim Brotherhood is an Islamist transnational movement and political opposition organization founded in Egypt in 1928 and active in many Arab states. Its focus was the establishment of an Islamic state—by any means, including extremely violent measures and corrupt methods of interfering in Sudan's political structure. The Brotherhood, which gained significant influence in the late 1970s, viewed the Addis Ababa Agreement as an unacceptable surrender of the Muslim North to the Christian and animist South.

By 1980, following threats and pressure from the Muslim Brotherhood, President Numeri be-

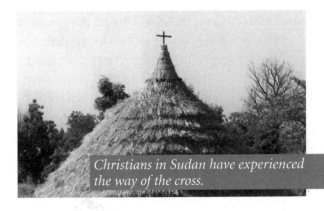

*Christians in Sudan have experienced the way of the cross.*

gan to present himself not as a military or socialist leader but as an Islamic leader. In 1983, in open hostility against all non-Muslims, President Numeri canceled the Peace Accord signed in 1972 and imposed Shariah (Islamic) Law, sparking the second civil war in Sudan. Sudan was now an even more deadly and dangerous den for those who refused to embrace Islam, and Christians faced new and brutal challenges for following Christ. In 1985, Muslim Brotherhood leader Hassan Turabi renamed his faction of the Brotherhood the National Islamic Front.

Twenty-two years of war followed the canceling of the Peace Accord. In this hostile time, the government of Sudan would be consistently involved in ethnic cleansing, wiping out entire villages and preventing aid from reaching war-torn areas. The government's aggression was also related to their desire for a newly discovered natural resource: oil. With the discovery of the precious and costly oil in Southern Sudan, the clashes increased in scope as the government sought to control this vast source of wealth. Using money from the oil industry that was developed by Western companies, the government purchased weapons in increasing number and sophistication to use against the Southern people.

The implementation of Shariah—also referred to as the "September Laws"—into Sudan's criminal code meant that new and severe punishments could be imposed indiscriminately on the public. One such penalty allowed was the amputation of limbs for theft and violent crime. While Islamic leaders claimed the law would affect only Muslims, it quickly became apparent that Southerners, particularly Christians, were being targeted in especially severe and brutal punishments.

Sudanese Christians did raise an outcry against Shariah Law, with churches from many denominations issuing statements and speaking up about the gross human rights violations being carried out against followers of Christ. However, church leaders were also vocal about encouraging fellow Christians to hold firm to their faith in Christ, even in this often terrifying time.

Christians were routinely arrested, interrogated, and tortured by Muslim officials in an attempt to convert them to Islam by force. Some bowed to the pressure, including two Christian men in a small village in the Nuba Mountains in 1993. The officials held the men for four days, denying them food or water, and repeatedly threatening to kill them if they did not embrace Islam, while promising them immediate release if they complied. On the fourth day, officers took the believers to a mosque where they succumbed to the pressure. The officers then gave each of the men 1,000 Sudanese pounds and a copy of the Qur'an and brought them safely back to their village.

The story of these two Christians is but one of many regarding followers of Christ in this time of war; many believers did stand firm, refusing to deny Christ even amid extreme pressure and painful torture. Some Christians, especially those who had come from a Muslim background, were reportedly even crucified.

In the second civil war, many churches and Christian relief agencies were often targeted in violence, including the highly regarded Nugent School in the city of Loka. In 2001, Islamic government soldiers attacked the Christian secondary school, leaving it in ruins before fleeing the area. The school and campus, founded by British missionaries in the mid-twentieth century, was at one time home to twenty-five hundred students, many of whom went on to become pastors, bishops, and government leaders. In June 2003, government-led military forces attacked ten villages in the Eastern Upper Nile of Sudan, killing the region's only Christian pastor, Jacob Manyal, and abducting his wife and two children. They also massacred at least fifty-nine unarmed villagers, wounded fifteen others, and abducted other women and children. Pastor Manyal's two children died while in the custody of government officials.

Many mosques were built during the second civil war, and churches demolished. When a mosque was built on unclaimed land in Sudan, that land was considered community property. In April 2003, Reverend Samuel Dobai Amu was sent to prison for refusing to demolish a church built on the outskirts of Khartoum. Officials told him that he must either destroy the church, which he had built eleven years earlier, or pay 7 million Sudanese dinars. He was unable to come up with such a large sum of money and said he could not demolish a house built in God's name.

The September 11, 2001, terrorist attacks on America drew more international attention to militant Islam, thus intensifying pressure on the Islamic government of Sudan to take part in peace talks. One of the main topics of negotiation in these peace talks in Sudan was the implementation of Shariah for non-Muslims. In July 2002, a historic peace deal was signed in Machakos, Kenya, between the government of Sudan and the Sudan People's Liberation Movement. That document, called the "Machakos Protocol," was a commitment to a negotiated, peaceful, comprehensive resolution to the Sudan conflict. An important element was its granting to the South the right to hold an internationally supervised referendum to determine independence after a six-year interim period beginning in July 2005. Five more proto-

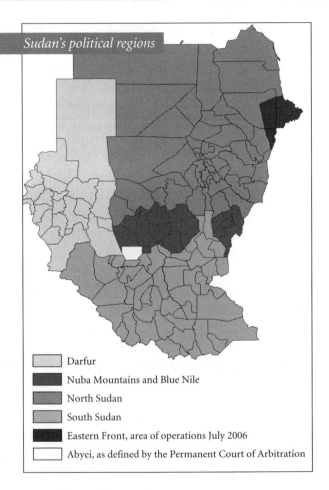

Sudan's political regions

Darfur

Nuba Mountains and Blue Nile

North Sudan

South Sudan

Eastern Front, area of operations July 2006

Abyei, as defined by the Permanent Court of Arbitration

cols followed, regarding security arrangements
(2003), wealth-sharing (2004), power-sharing
(2004), the resolution of conflict in southern Kor-
dofan/Nuba Mountains and the Blue Nile States

(2004), and the resolution of conflict in Abyei (2004).

Finally, in January 2005, a long-term peace accord, the "Naivasha Agreement" (also called the "Comprehensive Peace Accord"), was signed between the Sudan People's Liberation Movement and the Government of Sudan. Under this agreement, a referendum was to be held six years later to determine if South Sudan would gain full independence. It was a permanent cease-fire between the Southern rebels and the mostly Muslim government. July 6, 2005, was another historic day in the advance of religious freedom in Sudan, as Sudan's National Assembly passed a new constitution, stepping back from full Islamic rule. Under the new constitution, Islam was recognized as the majority religion in the country, but the existence and role of Christianity and traditional religions were also acknowledged. John Garang, former head of the SPLM rebel movement in South Sudan, was sworn in as vice-president and took leadership of the autonomous administration running the affairs of the predominantly Christian and animist Southern region of Sudan.

Sudan's civil war had been brought to an end. But the number of lives lost was astounding—nearly two million people, many of them Christians. Yet also astounding were the testimonies of steadfast faith—of Christians who, even without food or shelter or any guarantee of safety, still proclaimed their Savior's name during the second civil war. This resilience can be seen in many of the stories carried back by those who were able to visit South Sudan in this time. Even those who met with believers for but a few days, or even minutes, could see that their hope was in the Lord. When the Archbishop of Canterbury, George Carey, visited the Southern capital city of Juba in October 1995, he delivered these words to a crowd of tens of thousands of Sudanese Christians:

> If there is one thing that stands out in our experience of the Sudanese Church, it is that even though the problems are enormous, the wounds so deep, still Sudanese love and praise their God. Perhaps it is only truly because "God is your only strength and hope, a very present help in trouble." It is that confidence and joy which flows from it which you Sudanese bring to the worldwide Church...If our first impressions of Sudan may be tragedy, our last impressions are of the triumph of Christ crucified and raised from the dead.[4]

These sentiments contain the truth of Sudan's second civil war: it was not just a time of atrocities

---

4 Canon James M. Rosenthal, "Archbishop of Canterbury's Juba Cathedral Address," October 9, 1995, *Worldwide Faith News*. <www.wfn.org/1996/05/msg00710.html>. Accessed June 30, 2011.

and affliction, but also a period in which the glory of God's faithfulness was revealed. And so, even as the Sudanese Church looked ahead into an uncertain future, their country suffering the loss of millions of lives, they knew they had also been given a great opportunity to bear witness to the redeeming power of Christ. They knew He had not forgotten them, and His eternal peace, His shalom, would carry them, from the peace agreement and beyond.

## A PRAYER FOR THE
## MARTYRS OF SUDAN

*A liturgy written in 1983, following the declaration of Shariah Law in Sudan:*

O God, steadfast in the midst of persecution, by whose providence the blood of the martyrs is the seed of the Church: As the martyrs of the Sudan refused to abandon Christ even in the face of torture and death, and so by their sacrifice brought forth a plenteous harvest, may we, too, be steadfast in our faith in Jesus Christ; who with thee and the Holy Spirit liveth and reigneth, one God, for ever and ever. Amen.[5]

---

5 *Holy Women, Holy Men: Celebrating the Saints* (New York: Church Publishing Inc., 2010), p. 371.

## SUDAN TODAY:
## "I KNEW GOD WAS WITH ME"

The guards picked up a burning log from the fire.

"We will burn you and cut you until you become a Muslim," they said to Philip and his friends.

Philip had been taken to a military barracks along with thirty-five other Christians, both men and women.

For eleven days, Philip and his friends were bound, beaten, and burned as government soldiers tried to convert them to the Islamic faith. None of the twelve women survived the torture.

Philip still bears the scars on his chest left by the burning log used to torture him. He later told reporters, "My faith was very strong when they burned me. I prayed, 'God, I will never forget You.' I refused to be a Muslim because I knew God was with me."

# THE NUBA MOUNTAINS: GENOCIDE IN THE CENTER OF SUDAN

They are a sight of enormous beauty. Lying in the heart of the nation, the Nuba Mountains split North and South Sudan, stretching over an area roughly 40 miles wide by 90 miles long and towering 1,500 to 3,000 feet above the surrounding plain. And yet, this terrain of rugged loveliness has seen some of the ugliest violence in all of Sudan. The blood of Christians has been spilled in this lush landscape. Its people are acquainted with grief. They are also passionately acquainted with the fortifying glory and lovingkindness of the Lord.

For centuries, the people of the Nuba Mountains lived in peace and unity, even in their religious and cultural relationships. The Nuba people, descendants of an indigenous population located in what is now North Sudan, were driven into the mountains by advancing Arab tribes in A.D. 600. Known for their ethnic and religious diversity, they are a people rich in cultural customs that have been birthed as a result. They are composed of fifty ethnic groups and have roots in three religions: Islam, Christianity, and animism. It was not uncommon for members of all three religions to live peaceably within the same household.

The beginning of the second civil war, however, ushered in a new era of conflict for the Nuba people at the hands of Arab Muslims—most of them from nomadic tribes, armed by the government of Khartoum. When the battle between the Christian and animist South and the Muslim North broke out in 1983, the Nuba people forged an alliance with the Sudan People's Liberation Movement.

For many centuries, the Nuba Mountain region was shared peacefully with Arab traders. In the 1970s and 1980s Arab militias systematically seized the land of the Nuba people in an effort to prevent the forces of the Southern People's Liberation Army from reaching the North. It was a devastating blow, with the displacement furthering the feelings of vulnerability and powerlessness among the people.

Also during this time, Islamic officials in Khartoum were worried by their lack of political hold on the Nuba Mountains and sought to limit the growth of the Church. The officials pressured local chiefs, sometimes bribing them, to inform them about Christians in their area and then threatened to burn down churches. This pressure led young people to distrust local leaders and see them as doing the work of the Arabs, and many of them joined the SPLM. In 1983, the first church leader in the Nuba Mountain region was killed—a man named Paola Aldan. A wave of bloody attacks on church leaders and Christian schoolteachers then erupted, and several were killed or tortured. The violence led a number of Christians to flee to the South, and, in many cases, continue to swell the ranks of the SPLM.

In August 1985, the Muslim government began a campaign of burning churches through the mountains, including a church in Um Duru, where four Christians were killed in the attack. Muslims arrested Agnostino el-Nur Ibraham, a Christian teacher, and tortured him for a week, tying him with ropes and chains and beating and lashing him. "Quit being a Christian and close your church," they demanded. He was then transferred to Kadugli, a capital city located in the Nuba Mountains, where he was detained for four months. Muslims soldiers demanded that Agnostino repent and say Christianity was "a religion for foreigners" and "a religion of infidels." They tried to frighten him into converting by threatening to kill him if he did not embrace Islam, which would leave his children fatherless. One Muslim officer even offered him money and a house in Khartoum if he changed his religion. He was forced to go without food or water for days, hoisted up, spat upon, and had his genitals tortured with pliers. Angered by Agnostino's failure to renounce his faith in Christ, the guards eventually tied him up in a cross-like formation, in a kind of mock crucifixion. "How I managed to get out of their hands, I still don't know," Agnostino said. "It was a kind of miracle."

In 1985, the Nuba people were told to register their arms so that they would be given ammunition in order to defend themselves. It was a trick, however, and weapons were given only to Arab Muslims in the area. A stream of armed assaults, mostly on those without means to defend themselves, then ensued, with Arab Muslims stealing cattle and forcibly disarming the population.

In July 1988, Lubi, the most prominent Christian village in the Nuba Mountains, was attacked and completely burned down. Such attacks soon became commonplace, proving the Muslim aggression had reached a violent boiling point in the Nuba area.

In April 1992, a *fatwa* (Islamic ruling) was declared by the Khartoum government, providing a legal basis for the government's *jihad* against the Nuba people. The document stated: "Any insurgent who was previously a Muslim is now an apostate; and a non-Muslim is a non-believer standing as a bulwark against the spread of Islam, and Islam has granted the freedom of killing both of them." An unprecedented onslaught of military violence was unleashed on the population, including aerial bombings of marketplaces and villages. The Episcopal Church in the Nuba Mountains was also targeted in the mid-1990s when government forces burned down over twenty-five churches and murdered at least five clergymen. By early 1996, there were only seven Episcopalian pastors and seventy-two churches left in the SPLA-controlled regions of the Nuba Mountains.

During the second civil war, the people of the Nuba Mountains were cut off from food and aid as famines ravaged the nation. In the late 1980s, al-Bashir had agreed to a cease-fire with the South and permitted the United Nations to bring aid to the civilian population in the areas under SPLM administration. This aid arrangement excluded the Nuba Mountains, however, and the government army continued to deliberately target the Nuba people for decades. Schools and hospitals were also closed down, compounding their suffering.

On March 4, 1997, a team with members from Frontline Fellowship (a South African organization that serves persecuted Christians) and The Voice of the Martyrs was attacked by government helicopter gunships while delivering aid to the Nuba Mountains.

In January 2002, a ceasefire was negotiated between the Sudan government and the SPLA in

# SUDAN

Burgenstock, Switzerland. In 2005, when the Comprehensive Peace Agreement was drawn, the Nuba Mountains won special autonomous status—a distinction welcomed by the people there as a sign of stability in their region.

It would seem natural for the Nuba people to resist the added danger of professing Christ in this climate of crisis and violence. And yet, remarkably, people continued to come to Christ in record numbers during the years of the civil war. In a bold demonstration of faith against *jihad*, many even placed large crosses on their homes!

And the saga of suffering in this beautiful land is not yet over. In 2011, aerial bombardment and violence began again in the mountains. As in the early 1990s, the Arab Islamic forces in Khartoum closed the Nuba Mountains off from all humanitarian aid in an effort to wipe out the Nuba people. The sounds and sights of genocide returned to the mountains, renewing the risks especially for those who claim Christ boldly and unwaveringly, refusing to give in to the grip of the Islamists. "Once again," lamented the Bishop Andudu Adam Elnail of the Episcopal Diocese of Kadugli, "we are facing the nightmare of genocide of our people, a final attempt to erase our culture and society from the face of the earth."

Still, even in such times, there are those in the Nuba Mountains seeking the face of Christ and the hope of heaven. Today there remains a considerable Christian community in this region —many who came to Christ during tumultuous and tragic years of the past, finding liberation and comfort in the Lord, as well as new believers daring to follow Him even as bombs rain down. Theirs are the voices that advocates are seeking to share with the world—with the Church in Sudan and beyond. And their stories are stories not merely of violence, but of victory, which make plain the powerful heritage of Nuba Christians: faithfulness to the Lord in all and above all.

## SUDAN TODAY:
## MORE THAN A CONQUEROR
## THROUGH CHRIST

Abraham Yac Deng stood at the front of an Episcopal church in the village of Ayen in South Sudan. Over four hundred Christians were gathered, waiting eagerly to hear Abraham, a deacon, preach God's Word. They watched as Abraham reached into his shirt pocket. Slowly, with extreme care, he pulled out a Bible—the only one among the entire congregation. The book was tattered and faded, but one page looked especially worn. On this page was Romans chapter 8. Abraham read aloud verses 35–39, sharing that they had brought him particular comfort and peace.

The next month, in April 1998, The Voice of the Martyrs delivered a shipment of relief aid to the village, including six hundred Bibles. Abraham was overjoyed. At last his brothers and sisters would have their own copies of God's Word! There was no way Abraham could have anticipated what would happen next. Just a few weeks later, troops from the Na-

*Abraham Yac Deng*

tional Islamic Front stormed the area, attacking local believers. The Episcopal Church in Ayen was destroyed. Abraham was shot and killed. A pastor of the church and another deacon narrowly escaped death, while women and children were abducted to be sold as slaves. The Bibles, which had just arrived and had brought such joy to the community, were set ablaze and destroyed. What tragedy, what loss for these brothers and sisters! Yet Abraham Yac Deng's hope in the Lord blazed on; it could not be extinguished.

Today, the words that inspired Abraham continue to encourage our brothers and sisters in Sudan who are suffering for their faith in Christ:

> Who shall separate us from the love of Christ? Shall tribulation, or distress, or persecution, or famine, or nakedness, or peril, or sword? As it is written: "For Your sake we are killed all day long; we are accounted as sheep for the slaughter." Yet in all these things we are more than conquerors through Him who loved us. For I am persuaded that neither death nor life, nor angels nor principalities nor powers, nor things present nor things to come, nor height nor depth, nor any other created thing, shall be able to separate us from the love of God which is in Christ Jesus our Lord. (Romans 8:35–39)

# THE CRISIS IN DARFUR: A CHRISTIAN PERSECUTION ISSUE?

While the war between North and South Sudan has certainly gained more media coverage in recent decades, the region of Darfur, West Sudan, has been arguably more prominent in the central media.

The conflict in Darfur is between the Janjaweed, a government-supported militia recruited from local Arab tribes, and the black African peoples of the region. While the conflict has a political basis, it has also acquired an ethnic dimension as civilians were deliberately targeted on the basis of their ethnicity (which is why the term "ethnic cleansing" is correct).

It began in early 2003 after local rebel groups, the Justice and Equality Movement (JEM) and the Sudanese Liberation Army (SLA), who had long accused the government of oppressing black Africans in favor of Arabs, attacked government forces and installations. The SLA is not to be confused with the SPLA. Originally founded as the Darfur Liberation Front, the SLA grew specifically out of the Darfur conflict and consists of members from three ethnic groups. The government, caught by surprise by their attack, had very few troops in the region—and with a large proportion of them of Darfur origin, the government found itself unsure whether its own units could even be trusted. So in response it recruited an Arab militia from local tribes and armed them, mounting a campaign of aerial bombardment supported by ground attacks. In their quest to drive the two rebel groups from the Darfur region, these militias, backed by the government in Khartoum, have looted and burned homes, and raped, enslaved, and slaughtered scores of Sudanese. When news of this crisis began to circulate in 2003, however, some wondered if this conflict was connected to the oppression of South Sudan by the North—and many questioned the religious aspect. Some Christians, especially those aware of the oppression of Christ's followers in the country, wondered if there was a religious element to the horrendous conflict—a genocide which has lead to the death of at least 200,000 to 400,000 and displaced approximately 2.5 million Sudanese. Could this be a persecution issue?

Although there are Christians in Darfur, the crisis itself only indirectly affects them. They may suffer from violent attacks or oppressive treatment, but these are more related to their ethnic identity than their religious identity. If they were to convert to Islam, they would likely still be targeted in the same manner due to their ethnicity and economic status.

This is not to say, however, that Christians should not continue to pray for, and seek ways to support, the people of Darfur. Despite suffering intense persecution at the hands of militant Muslims and the challenges of ethnic tension, Sudanese Christians reportedly continue to reach out to Muslims, including the refugees in the bordering areas of Darfur, with the Good News of the gospel. Theirs is a commitment to sharing the grace and love of Christ that should be lived out and echoed by Christ's Body worldwide.

## A FRAGILE PEACE:
## SOUTH SUDAN'S SECESSION

It was early morning, just a few hours after midnight. Voters were already gathered at the polls. Some were singing and chanting slogans—words of hope that this day, January 9, 2011, would begin a move toward the independence of South Sudan from the North after a prolonged period of civil war.

This day had been long coming. In 2005, the government in Khartoum and the South Sudan People's Liberation Movement had signed a peace agreement that ended the country's bitter civil war. This agreement established semi-autonomy in the South and called for a referendum on independence six years later. After years of waiting, the polls opened on January 9.

It is possible that Christian voters went to the polls with the widely reported threat of President Omar al-Bashir ringing in their ears—words of warning over what could happen in the aftermath of the vote. "If South Sudan secedes, we will change the constitution," President al-Bashir said. "Shariah and Islam will be the main source for the constitution—Islam the official religion and Arabic the official language." In the days surrounding the vote, many Northern Christians reportedly fled to the South out of fear that President al-Bashir's regime will shift toward "radical Islamization" in the wake of the referendum.

Just a little over a week later, on January 14, the voting process came to an end. It was decided: South Sudan would in fact become the world's newest nation. Many greeted the news with great joy, seeing it as an answer to prayer. Yet, as many Sudanese Christians noted, it was also a cause to renew the fervent call for intercessory prayer as they looked forward to July 9, the day of official secession. According to one church leader in South Sudan, Eduardo Hiiboro Kussala of Tombura-Yambio, many Sudanese Christians have strong "expectations of change for the better." He also urged continued prayers worldwide for "permanent peace in Sudan." This emphasis on prayer is evidence of the faithful reliance on God that has characterized the Sudanese Church for centuries.

The last months leading up to the succession were filled with alarming developments for the people of Sudan, with violent clashes in several provinces and increased violence in the western region of Darfur. In the border town of Abyei, a referendum was delayed and attempts to assert military control erupted in violence. Government agents and Islamic militants launched deadly attacks on Christians in Sudan's South Kordofan state, looting churches and raiding the area in search of Christians. In another region, Sudan Armed Forces (SAF) shot and killed a seminary student in front of several bystanders, claiming that he opposed the Islamic government. Islamic militants aligned with SAF also attacked a church building, shooting at the Christians gathered inside. Although no one was injured in the attack, agents detained the pastor, Reverend Abraham James, torturing him for two days for allegedly preaching that people should oppose the Islamic government.

Thousands of people were displaced and forced to flee to the South in the wake of these attacks. With Christians continuing to flee, fear has also increased that those who remained would be especially vulnerable to future pressure and violence.

As of this printing, the milestone day of July 9 has come and gone, and South Sudan is fresh into its new chapter of independence. Around the world, political figures, Christian leaders, and others congratulated the world's youngest nation. But for those on either side of the new border, many challenges remain—such as President Omar Al-Bashir's intentions of adopting an Islamic constitution and bolstering Shariah (Islamic law) to reflect the north's 98 percent Muslim majority. All the while, prayers for permanent peace for the Sudanese people continue to be lifted up. Still

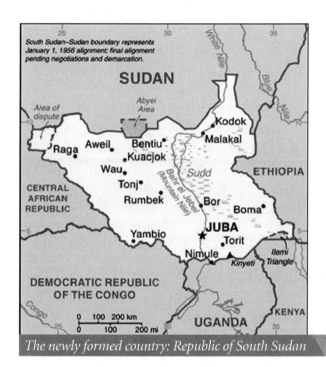

> South Sudan–Sudan boundary represents January 1, 1956 alignment; final alignment pending negotiations and demarcation.

*The newly formed country: Republic of South Sudan*

Sudan's people long for true and lasting unity. Still God's faithful children ask God to enable their witness to be made stronger, not weaker, by pressure and potential violence. Still Christ watches over this land, reigning in all His glory, authority, and sovereignty.

May the Church in both of these nations continue, together, to build on the century-long legacy of forsaking all in loving loyalty to Jesus Christ.

# CONCLUSION:
## AFFLICTED BUT
## NOT FORGOTTEN

A passage about the coming Messiah being afflicted, slain, and deprived of justice (Isaiah 53) was the Word that spoke to the heart of the eunuch, the first Christian in the Sudanese area. Ironically (or, one may say, providentially), this chapter from what theologians call "The Songs of the Suffering Servant" fits with the sufferings Sudanese Christians have experienced in both the past and present.

In today's Sudan, it is still dangerous to be a Christian. Christians in North Sudan are subject to many of the restrictions facing believers in other Muslim countries. Evangelism is allowed by law but still fiercely opposed by the government and thus very limited. Many Christian converts from Islam also face intense pressure and harassment from their own family members, with some fleeing the country or going into hiding as a result. Apostasy (leaving Islam) is punishable by death. Violation of Section 125 of the Sudanese Criminal Act, which prohibits "insulting religion, inciting hatred and showing contempt for religious beliefs," is punishable by imprisonment of one year, a fine, and forty lashes. While convictions are reportedly rare, Christian converts from Islam continue to be victims of Sudan's blasphemy law.

Believers are rarely granted visas for humanitarian and missionary work; those who are experience significant delays. Both Christians and animists face intense pressure to convert to Islam. Christian leaders have been jailed and beaten simply for meeting with people interested in coming to Christ.

The gospel is going forward in Sudan, even in this climate of instability and oppression. Thirty years of persecution has not stopped the growth of the Sudanese Church. Most expatriate missionaries have left, but national leaders remain committed to evangelism. Life continues to be difficult as the country struggles for stability, but pastors are begging for Bibles and Christian training items rather than material aid. In today's Sudan, many Christians, like the apostle Philip, are eagerly welcoming others joining in the precious league of the faithful.

For many years, The Voice of the Martyrs has been active in Sudan, letting the Body of Christ know that it is not forgotten. VOM has delivered medical care, special Christmas gift packages, and even blankets to show warmth and love to believers in a uniquely tangible way. VOM has also part-

*Help arrives in Sudan.*

nered with the ministry Global Response Network in assisting with the Nugent School in Loka, South Sudan. This Christian school was rebuilt after it was destroyed in years of war and now serves to help rebuild a country and Church that have been wracked by violence.

*The Nugent School in Loka*

# SUDAN

Our Sudanese family members in Christ need to be remembered before the throne of our Lord. Pray for God to give believers in all regions of Sudan wisdom as they navigate the days ahead in a time of transition. Pray that their witness will remain strong and that they will continue to shine the light of the Lord in a nation where there is still much injustice and pain. Pray they will know that the Church around the world is standing with them as they build and rebuild their nation on the foundation of Christ's love and grace. Pray that they will heed His guidance in their lives as they serve Him. Pray that the image of Christ, a righteous sufferer and redeemer, will be bright on their hearts and minds.

And as a member of Christ's flock, will you speak for these brothers and sisters in Sudan? Will you ask the Lord to equip and guide you as to how you might intercede so that they will not suffer in silence? Pray that these devoted servants be aware that their cries are heard, by their Father and by their Christian family worldwide. May they know that even while they may be humiliated, deprived of justice—even killed—their stories and witness do not go untold. May they sense the presence of a Shepherd who hears their cries. And may they know that even if they are afflicted, they are not, and will never be, forgotten.

# FOR FURTHER READING

*The following sources, a selection of those consulted in the writing of this book, are recommended for further reading and research.*

DC Talk with The Voice of the Martyrs. 1999. *Jesus Freaks: Stories of Those Who Stood for Jesus: The Ultimate Jesus Freaks*. Tulsa, OK: Albury Publishing.

Hammond, Peter. 1998. *Faith under Fire in Sudan*. Newlands, South Africa: Frontlines Fellowship.

Heyboer, Marvin W. 2009. *Journeys into the Heart and Heartland of Islam*. Pittsburgh, PA: Dorrance Publishing Co., Inc.

Jok, Madut Jok. 2007. *Sudan: Faith, Religion and Violence*. Oxford, England: Oneworld Publications.

Levi, William O. 2005. *The Bible or the Axe*. Chicago: Moody Publishers.

Marshall, Paul. 2007. *Religious Freedom in the World*. Nashville, TN: Rowman & Littlefield Publishers, Inc.

Marshall, Paul. 1997. *Their Blood Cries Out: The Untold Story of Persecution Against Christians*. Dallas, TX: Word Publishing.

Meyer, Gabriel and James Nicholls. 2005. *War and Faith in Sudan*. Grand Rapids, MI: William B. Eerdmans Publishing.

Nikkel, Marc R. 2001. *Dinka Christianity: The Origins and Development of Christianity Among the Dinka of Sudan*. Nairobi: Paulines Publications Africa.

Preller, Arnoldus Mauritius. "Present and future challenges to the church in Africa—with special reference to the church in Sudan." University of Pretoria: Electronic Theses and Dissertations. <http://dcommon-test.bu.edu/xmlui/handle/2144/901>. Accessed December 23, 2010.

Strom, Kay Marshall and Michele Ricket. 2003. *Daughters of Hope: Stories of Witness and Courage in the Face of Persecution*. Downers Grove, IL: InterVarsity Press.

Werner, Roland, William Anderson, and Andrew Wheeler. 2000. *Day of Devastation, Day of Contentment: The History of the Sudanese Church Across 2000 Years*. Nairobi: Paulines Publications Africa.

Wheeler, Andrew C., ed. 1998. *Announcing the Light: Sudanese Witnesses to the Gospel*. Nairobi: Paulines Publications Africa.

Wheeler, Andrew C. "Christianity in Sudan." *Dictionary of African Christian Biography*. <www.cb.

org/history/christianity in sudan.html>. Accessed
June 4, 2010.

## Other Resources

The Barnabas Fund: www.barnabasfund.org

The Voice of the Martyrs monthly newsletter and
websites:

    www.persecution.com (USA)
    www.persecution.net (Canada)

The Frontline Fellowship: www.frontline.org.za

Compass Direct: www.compassdirect.org

# RESOURCES

The Voice of the Martyrs has many books, videos, brochures, and other products to help you learn more about the persecuted church. In the U.S., to request a resource catalog, order materials, or receive our free monthly newsletter, call (800) 747-0085 or write to:

The Voice of the Martyrs
P.O. Box 443
Bartlesville, OK 74005-0443
www.persecution.com
thevoice@persecution.com

If you are in Australia, Canada, New Zealand, South Africa, or the United Kingdom, contact:

**Australia:**
>   Voice of the Martyrs
>   P.O. Box 250
>   Lawson NSW 2783
>   Australia
>
>   Website: www.persecution.com.au
>   Email: thevoice@persecution.com.au

**Canada:**
>   Voice of the Martyrs, Inc.
>   P.O. Box 608

Streetsville, ON L5M 2C1
Canada

Website: www.persecution.net
Email: thevoice@persecution.net

## New Zealand:

Voice of the Martyrs
P.O. Box 5482
Papanui, Christchurch 8542
New Zealand

Website: www.persecution.co.nz
Email: thevoice@persecution.co.nz

## South Africa:

Christian Mission International
P.O. Box 7157
1417 Primrose Hill
South Africa

Email: cmi@icon.co.za

## United Kingdom:

Release International
P.O. Box 54
Orpington BR5 9RT
United Kingdom

Website: www.releaseinternational.org
Email: info@releaseinternational.org